MONSTERS

1. Sea monsters were big in Norse mythology. This ancient woodcut shows a struggle between one of them and the Teutonic god, Thor.

MONSTERS

THEIR HISTORIES, HOMES, AND HABITS

BY PERLE EPSTEIN

7/7³

*398
E*

Blairsville Junior High School
Blairsville, Pennsylvania

DOUBLEDAY & COMPANY, INC.

GARDEN CITY, NEW YORK

ISBN: 0-385-01414-7 Trade
0-385-04874-2 Prebound
Library of Congress Catalog Card Number 72–97496
Copyright © 1973 by Perle Epstein
ALL RIGHTS RESERVED
Printed in the United States of America
First Edition

For Sarah Besserman, my darling niece.

CONTENTS

MONSTERS

2. Prester John—the mythical priest-king of the Middle Ages. He was a world traveler, and Prester John's land was named for him.

PREFACE

Monsters are useful creatures. They guard treasures, amuse and protect kings, frighten the wits out of nosy travelers, allow heroes to win the hearts of ladies, and, on occasion, disclose the secrets of the universe to courageous wise men.

Natural historians would have it that "monsters" are really nothing more than extinct creatures that have been decorated by mythmakers and artists. Show us a *dragon*, they say, and we'll trace him back to the Lacertilian, a twenty-foot-long creature covered in terrifying armor that roamed across Australia during the Pleistocene period. Add to this the fact that the ancients called all snakes dragons and peppered them with nearly every nasty trait they could think of; stir in a tablespoon of anthropology (whose maiden-devouring dragons are appeased in exchange for a fruitful harvest); and you have the birth of a monster.

Sir John Mandeville, a popular voyager of the Middle Ages, disagrees. In typically no-nonsense medieval fashion, he says: "A monster is a thing deformed against kind both of man or of beast or of anything else, and that is called a monster." According to his own delightful first-, and sometimes third-hand accounts, most of these creatures inhabit the Arabian desert, or the magical land of Prester John (located somewhere near Africa or India); otherwise, they can be found roaming the wilds of Ethiopia. These are very convenient monster habitats since Sir John's European audience was not usually given to distant travel, and the more fantastic the accounts, the better. To people who believed that to be pagan was to be a sort of monster anyway, there were many moral lessons to be learned from these bizarre events of nature, and *Bestiaries*—popular animal encyclopedias with a message—provided many an imaginative monk with a long day's copying.

Fear of strangers and faraway places made for a very real belief in monsters all the way from biblical times to the end of the eighteenth century. Even during such a scholarly age as the Renaissance, men continued to believe in the symbolic importance of monsters. Heaven and earth were spoken of as living organisms with hair, teeth, and bones. Giordano Bruno, an Italian mystic, saw the planets as warm-blooded, rational animals. Understandable perhaps in a mystic; but what of a scientist like Johannes Kepler, who saw the earth as a living monster "whose whalelike breathing, changing with sleep and wakefulness, produces the ebb and flow of the seas"?

In our own time, however, even a highly imaginative writer like Jorge Luis Borges can say with scientific aplomb: "A monster is no more than a combination of parts of real beings, and the possibilities of permutations border on the infinite."

We have reached the point, then, where monsters are strictly for fun.

3. The Cyclops were the one-eyed giants of Greek myth. The best known one is Polyphemus whose downfall began when Odysseus put out his eye. Here is a picture of the event as portrayed on an ancient Greek vase.

ONE

MONSTERS FOR
ENTERTAINMENT
AND PROTECTION

Throughout the history of the human race, the birth or sudden appearance of a monster, either human or animal, most frequently was forecast by unnatural signs, portents, or "prodigies." The word monster is derived from the Latin word meaning "to warn," and is generally associated with the wrath of God or, less frequently, with His approval. Monsters fall into the same category as comets and shooting stars.

To the Caesars, who read the entrails of animals for prophecy of things to come, a sheep with two stomachs might set an emperor to worrying about his future. In most cases, though, it depended on who was doing the interpreting, and on how tactful he or she chose to be about it.

The Greeks believed that monsters were the result

of the union between a god and a human being. Zeus, who had a way with mortal women, is said to have fathered many varieties of semihuman monsters. Twenty-eight hundred years before the birth of Christ, Babylonians credited the position of the stars with the appearance of monsters.

All early races believed in giants, some even going so far as to worship them. The Bible, for example, is populated with colossal human beings like *Nephilim*, *Rephaim*, and the *Anakim* of Hebron who were, according to Deuteronomy, "a people great and tall . . . who can stand before the children of Anak." Goliath, perhaps the most famous of the breed, represents only one of the many giants who were on the earth in those days. He stood six cubits and a span (9 feet, 9 inches) and wore a coat of mail weighing 208 pounds. Og, the king of Bashan, last of the biblical giants, had six fingers on each hand and six toes on each enormous foot.

Titans, the most popular of which is Polyphemus, the one-eyed *Cyclops* outsmarted by Ulysses, were Greek giants of enormous strength who battled against the gods and savored human flesh. Homer describes Polyphemus thus:

> A form enormous; far unlike the race
> of human birth, in stature or in face
> as some lone mountain's monstrous growth he stood,
> Crown'd with rough thickets and a nodding wood.

In the fourteenth century, Boccaccio writes of the

discovery in Sicily of the Cyclop's three hundred foot-long bones. A Jesuit named Kircher reassessed the skeleton's size and claimed that it was only thirty feet tall.

The Titans' wives gave birth to *Gigantes,* ugly creatures with frightful faces and dragons' tails, fifty heads, one hundred arms each, and serpents for legs. Hercules, himself a demi-god standing seven feet tall, conquered these monsters by crushing them to death under mountains or beating them down with clubs.

Traditionally, giants seem to exist in order to be killed off by heroes who are themselves taller than the average man and, of course, infinitely stronger. Within the realm of recorded time, we find the giant assuming a more practical function. During the Roman reign of Augustus Caesar, for example, the Guardians of Sallust were giants measuring ten feet, three inches each. These oversized men formed an elite guard for the protection of the emperor—an increasingly common practice, as we shall see.

Frequently, the height and strength of the emperor himself could be inflated for patriotic purposes. The Emperor Maximilian of Austria was noted to stand near nine feet in height. His shoe size extended a foot beyond that of other men, his daily meals included forty pounds of meat and six gallons of wine. Such strength and stamina did he possess that, despite this great stomachful of food, he could pull a wagon heavy enough to stall two oxen.

The French emperor Charlemagne matched Maximilian in size and strength; in fact, he went a step further and lived to be four hundred years old. But his private giant bodyguard, Aenotherus, was even larger than he, throwing down entire battalions "as he would have mowed grass." Charlemagne's nephew Roland made a name for himself by slaughtering Terragus, a monster standing eleven feet high.

The Scots, not to be outdone, have recorded the existence of an eleven-foot, six-inch giant who lived in the twelfth century during the reign of King Eugene the Second. Another huge Scottish monster, caught in 1490, possessed two sets of limbs. Brought up in the king's household, the half-male, half-female creature was taught music and languages. In addition, the monster developed the unique traits of disagreeing with itself, looking out with both faces in opposite directions, and singing double part harmony. Sometimes it disagreed with itself so fiercely as to come to blows.

The Welsh, not content to leave well enough alone, added two heads to *their* home-grown giant. *Spriggans*, or ghosts of giants, are still believed to inhabit the Cornwall coast of England as treasure guardians. And finally, in America, in 1705, the bones of a legendary Indian giant were found and measured to the length of a huge pine tree. According to Ezra Stiles, then president of Yale college, this creature would kill bears with his bare hands and catch four or five sturgeon at a time while wading into water twelve or fourteen feet deep. He was also reputed to be a gentle giant, who never hurt his smaller Indian brothers.

The subtle transformation of a mythical and heroic monster into a useful and entertaining one takes place somewhere between the early Middle Ages and the sixteenth century. But not always, unfortunately, to the benefit of the "monster" himself. Royal personages all over Europe indulged themselves in a little monster craze of sorts; giants were in special demand as porters, guards, janitors, and soldiers. Queen Elizabeth's own gateman was seven feet, six inches. The empress of Austria collected an entire gathering of giants and dwarfs in order to satisfy her own jaded curiosity. Contemporary accounts of this incident portray the cruelty that often accompanied the whims of royalty. According to one, all the empress' giants and dwarfs were bundled together in one building, where—to everyone's surprise—the tiny people tortured and robbed the miserable giants.

Contrary to the old heroic and mythical accounts, historical giants have been found to be gentle, easily bullied, and none too clever. Because of their obvious physical advantages in a tumultuous age, giants enjoyed a resurgence of soldierly interest during the eighteenth century. The king of Prussia formed for himself an elite squadron of gigantic guards—the first in Europe. Armed with a huge sergeant's cane, King Frederick amused himself by performing daily reviews of his supersquadron who were each no

Victoria and Albert Museum

4. Giants have been a part of the folklore of all countries. Remember Jack and the Beanstalk?

less than seven feet, whose nationalities ranged from European to Asian, and whose cost was presumably as great as their size.

Nevertheless, it was more often as "monstrosities" than as respected warriors that giants were employed. The cruel and inhuman example of the Austrian empress could be found scattered about on public handbills advertising the many popular male and female giants of the period:

> Tall Woman of seven foot and three inches high. Weighs 415 pounds, who has had the honour to be shown before Seven Kings in Europe.

From the sixteenth through the eighteenth centuries, the "strong man" abounded as a popular form of carnival entertainment. One such, a singing strong *lady*, would sing a song as she propped a platform—piano, pianist, and all—upon her shoulders. Sevententh-century England showed a particular taste for entertainment like the "hairy woman" seen by Sir John Evelyn, and noted in his diary for September 15, 1651:

> Her very eyebrows were combed upwards and all her forehead as thick and even as growes on any woman's head, neatly dressed.

> A very long lock of hair out of each ear. She also had a most prolix beard and mustachios, with long locks growing on ye middle of the nose, like an Iceland dog exactly, the colour of a bright browne, fine as well-dressed flax. . . . She was very well-shaped and plaied well on ye harpsichord.

Monsters

Great or little size, odd features, superhuman strength, and masses of hair were traits to be exploited for the ghoulish delight of the mob. Monsters from distant lands particularly commanded a frenzy of popular acclaim. Some quickly learned to adapt and even to please by putting on grotesque performances. The "wild creature" from Bilboa, for example, thrust out his foot-long tongue, rolled his eyes in and out simultaneously, contracted his face, and extended his mouth six inches. He purportedly had the muscular flexibility to make a bird's beak of his lips, lick his nose with his tongue like a cow, and change the color of his skin to that of a corpse long dead. "Altho' bred wild so long yet by travelling with some comedians eighteen years, he can sing wonderfully fine and accompanies his voice with a thorrow bass on the lute," says one contemporary report.

Another showpiece, a female, had supposedly been taken from the jungles of Ethiopia via the Cape of Good Hope. Her entire body was described as partaking of familiar "human nature," except for a "long monstrous head." Her activities, on the other hand, had never been seen "in this part of the world before, she showing many strange and wonderful actions which gives great satisfaction to all that ever did see her."

Erik Pontoppidan, a Norwegian bishop, author of an exhaustive and fantastic *Natural History of Norway*, published in 1755, describes an African creature presented as a gift to Frederick Henry, prince of Orange. This "wood man," said to have been produced by mating a woman or man with an ape, is described as being the size of a three-year-old child and weighing as much as a six-year-old. It was strong, covered with rough hair, had a flat nose, human ears, protuberant breasts, a navel, and normal human limbs.

According to Pontoppidan, who was not above taking his rock-bound evidence from hearsay, "It frequently walked erect, and could take up a heavy weight, and bear it away. When it wanted to drink, it fixed one hand to the bottom of a tankard, and with the other took hold of the lid, and drank, wiping its lips afterwards. It laid its head regularly upon a pillow, when inclined to sleep, and covered itself carefully with the bedclothes."

The interesting question here is why the good bishop and his contemporaries chose to see a monster rather than a chimpanzee in this interesting royal gift. Why, in his conclusion, does Pontoppidan say, "this animal appears to be the Satyr of the ancients," rather than, "this animal is a baby monkey"? Could it be that the age of faith and fantasy had not yet been swallowed up by the age of science and practicality?

Dwarfs are characteristically clever and witty. Where giants, all brawn and no brain, have been used and mistreated for their size, history is filled with the success stories of sly and talented dwarfs.

25

Saxon legends portray four sacred dwarfs as the up-holders of Heaven itself—one at each corner of the universe. A contrary belief is that dwarfs, as creations of the Devil, were formed to promote mischief. Devilish methods can certainly be attributed to the monstrous craftsmen who created dwarfs by enclosing children in little pots and feeding them burned wine along with other growth-inhibiting concoctions.

Travelers in Central Africa, from the Romans on-ward have noted the activity and cunning of the pygmies in contrast to the obedient and generally slow-witted nature of giant tribesmen. While their larger brothers were bought as guardsmen and the like, it has been the fate of dwarfs to be kept as humorous pets, witty advisors, and court jesters in royal households. The ancient Egyptians likened them to the dwarf god, Ptah, and therefore revered them; the Romans decked out their naked dwarfs in magnificent jewels and then paraded them through the streets.

Alypius, one highly respected Alexandrian dwarf-philosopher, measured one foot, five inches, and was described as having "a kind of divine nature." Later, the Spanish painter Velasquez painted the dwarfs belonging to the Spanish court. Showered with precious gifts, these little people (often called "prodigies" during the sixteenth and seventeenth centuries) were freely exchanged by kings and queens all over Europe. The year 1566 sees Cardinal Vitelli of Italy giving a sumptuous Roman banquet served by thirty-four dwarfs dressed elegantly as waiters.

5. *One of the most famous dwarfs hanging around the royal court was Rumpelstiltskin. Here he is in a drawing by Cruickshank.*

Monsters

Zep, a dwarf reputed to possess occult powers, was bought in 1580 by Tycho Brahe, the famous Danish astronomer. So great were his talents, that Zep was brought into the homes of the sick to comment on the outcome of their illnesses.

Another, a tiny wise man from Verona named Bertholde, went so far as to be appointed Prime Minister to the king of Lombardy. He is described as being "a kind of monster," whose oversized head covered with coarse red hair, small ugly eyes, and enormous eyebrows were complemented by a grotesque body. His nose was big and wide, and his lips, though large enough, could hardly cover his tusklike teeth. A pendant lower lip and bristly beard completed the unfortunate features of his face. Bertholde was no less popular for his ugly appearance, however. Kings and diplomats took his wise advice very seriously, and though he suffered the typical ups and downs of a politician, he enjoyed the favors of the powerful, making his living by his wits to the end.

David Riccio, French secretary and musician to Mary Queen of Scots, is also described as having been singularly frightening in appearance—dwarfed and humped over. Yet the sweetness of his voice, the beauty of his musical compositions, his literacy and intellectual power made him stand out like a refined jewel from the circle of boorish lords that surrounded the queen. Riccio paid horribly for his royal successes; dragged from his queen's chamber in the midst of a card game, he was brutally stabbed and flung down the palace stairs by a group of jealous noblemen. In those turbulent times, the word monster evidently applied only to appearance and not to deeds.

In the eighteenth century, when verbal daggers had replaced the steel ones, and when one well-chosen public remark might devastate a man's reputation, if not his entire career at court, Alexander Pope, another humpbacked dwarf, achieved great public acclaim with his sly and sometimes bitter pen. It is the underlying bitterness in the jests of all these famous society "pets" that haunts their worldly successes. A well-dressed, well-paid monster is still a monster after all, a creature to be gawked at, fussed over, despised.

It was not until the late nineteenth century that the attitude toward these human "prodigies" changed from amusement to compassion. One such turning point occurs in the dramatic story of John Merrick, "the elephant man." London's Whitechapel Road, in the year 1888, provided the setting. Here, in a cold vacant shop, a carnival promoter was charging a shilling for a view of a "frightful creature." Dr. Frederick Treves, a surgeon, happened to be passing the shop when his eye was caught by the poster in the window. Once inside, he was granted his first introduction to the elephant man, a "thing" that even the enlightened doctor called "the most disgusting specimen of humanity that I have ever seen. . . ."

Ordered by the promoter to stand up, the creature revealed its distorted and oversized head and huge bony forehead "horn." Another spongy gathering of skin hung in a brownish mass from the back of his head. One eye was almost hidden, the hairs were sparse but long, the nose an unrecognizable lump, while the mouth barely covered another bony tusk. The poor creature was covered over with tumors and, as the doctor soon learned, suffered from a tuberculosis of the hip that emitted a foul odor.

It was an awful but scientifically fascinating sight, interesting enough for Dr. Treves to devote a paper to it and to label the phenomenon "Merrick's Disease." Two years later, however, the monster turned up again, this time at the Liverpool Street Station, where the police had rescued him from a violent mob. Appealing to the administrator of the London Hospital for space and to the readers of the *Times* for funds, Dr. Treves successfully installed Merrick in an isolated hospital room. Here he was given a bed, washed, fed, and allowed to "talk." Communication between the two men was difficult at first, for Merrick could only emit unintelligible sounds. But as time went by the doctor learned to understand them, and so obtained the story of the elephant man's life. To his surprise, he found Merrick to be an intelligent lover of books, sensitive, and almost saintly in his tolerance of the world's abuse.

Working in league with other sympathetic men and women, Dr. Treves gradually helped to draw

Merrick out of his shell of self-loathing. He managed to persuade attractive women visitors to smile and shake his patient's hand, and sometimes even arranged for him to visit the theater in a secluded seat. Like his fellow "monsters" of the past, Merrick, too, attracted the attention of royalty—but no longer as a titillating curiosity of nature. Princes sent him books, food, and decorations for his room, while elegant noblewomen, daring to look into his frightening face without so much as a shudder, came to talk with him. Under Dr. Treves's kindly and knowledgeable supervision, John Merrick lived on—as a human being rather than a monstrous freak—for three years more. He was never cured of his pathetic condition, but he gained recognition as a man.

Staatliche Kunsthalle Karlsruhe

John Webb

6. *This old woodcut shows a dragon breathing fire. The man in the picture is More of More Hall, dressed in armor studded with spikes, kicking the beast to death.*

TWO

DRAGONS, BASILISKS, AND VARIATIONS THEREOF

The true embodiment of evil has been and always will be the dragon. Satan, Anti-Christ, sin, all the natural and unnatural dangers of the universe live within this snaky figure.

"And the great dragon was cast out, that old serpent called the Devil, and Satan, which deceiveth the whole world: he was cast out into the earth, and his angels were cast out with him." The biblical monster referred to here was kept in a Babylonian temple until the hero Daniel killed it by sneaking it a pill made of hair and bitumen.

The guardian of the Greek Garden of the Hesperides, the *Hydra,* is also a vicious dragon whose sole occupation is to scare away anyone who might take it into his head to steal one of the golden apples growing there. No surprise then that in Greek, "dragon" means sharp-sighted one. Hydra has many heads, each possessing the power to regenerate itself after being cut off.

Monsters

Draco, the Latin word for dragon, means giant snake, or python. This creature was usually represented in classical art as a fire breather with large bat's wings, a monster who spent his time in dark caves and sea grottoes guarding treasures. Many people believed that dragon bones and dragon teeth had powerful curative effects, but few, presumably, ever had the chance to use them.

Of all the monsters, dragons are the most varied in type and appearance. Some have four legs, some two, while others have no legs at all. Sometimes dragons sprout wings; many have forked tongues—usually spitting poison fire. There are dragons with pointed tails, fringes, crests on their heads, scales on their bodies. They can be feathered, furred, or smooth. Basically, however, dragons are large, long, reptilian, and dangerous.

The number of their vicious limbs and appendages varies in accordance with the legend and symbolism of a particular society; the red dragon of the Apocalypse, for example, boasts seven heads, ten horns, and seven crowns on each of its seven heads. One medieval *Bestiary* speaks of dragons that are the special enemies of doves, an allegory for Christ and the Devil. Even the trees where doves live are dangerous, forcing dragons to avoid the shadows of their branches. Should an unwary dove find itself beyond the line of the tree's shade, however, the dragon will kill it. Draco is depicted in this *Bestiary* as bearing a crest and having a small mouth and a narrow gullet through which he breathes and thrusts out his tongue. He kills by flailing his thick tail rather than by stinging or spitting fire; at other times, he may choose to choke his victims with his tail instead.

Sirrush, the Babylonian dragon represented in the Ishtar gate erected by King Nebuchadnezzar, was used mainly to impress people with the king's strength and power. Grim and frightening, richly designed, Sirrush has scales, a long thin tail, and a neck that ends in a serpent's head. The forked tongue sticks out of a closed mouth, while a pointed horn completes the fearsome picture. To denote the physical appearance of the king himself, perhaps, the artists gave the dragon three corkscrew curls near the ears and a long set of curls at the neck. The front feet are those of a lion, the two rear feet are clawed—supposedly designed for digging the burrows where it lives. This great beast is immune to all weapons; a likely, if somewhat glorified figure of an ancient, conceited king.

To the Hebrews, and later to the Christians who were enslaved and oppressed by many kings like Nebuchadnezzar, the dragon came to be identified with everything loathsome and destructive. Guardian of all the worldly treasures which they, as slaves, could never hope to share, the dragon was regarded by these ancient peoples as the true enemy of man, a monster to be overcome and conquered.

Heathen nations, too, either battled the monster,

or worshipped him as a god full of dangerous physical force and irrational anger.

Propertius, a Latin writer, tells of a town twenty miles from Rome that always has been protected by an old dragon. In return for his services, the villagers must provide him with food served by a beautiful young maiden. Lowered into the slimy pit where he lives, the young woman must feed the monster with her own hands, never flinching as he snatches the food from her fingers in great gulps. If the girl is pure in body and in heart, she and her empty basket are returned safely to her family; embracing them, she cries: "We shall have a fruitful year!" The villagers do their utmost to find a *pure* maiden, you can be sure.

Pliny, the Roman natural historian, believed that "the dragon is a serpent destitute of venom; its head placed beneath the threshold of a door, the gods being duly propitiated by prayers, will ensure good fortune to the house . . ." In accordance with such accepted beliefs, Erictho, a famous Thessalian witch, used a dragon in order to resuscitate a corpse. (Brewed dragon, of course.) Dried dragon's eyes stirred into honey are said to be good antidotes for nightmares. The ingenious Pliny also recommended the skin of the *Amphisbena* as a remedy for cold shivers. This reptile wears one head on its neck and another in its tail. Putting its heads together, the Amphisbena "can bowl along in either direction like a hoop," and takes cold weather very well. Pregnant women are advised against stepping over this monster, however, for it brings on miscarriages.

Greek and Roman poets often put the dragon into their fables when they needed an easily recognized emblem of power, magic, and ferocity. Two such dragons licked the eyes of Plutus at the temple of Aesculapius and made him see again—another example of the common belief in a dragon's healing powers. This idea was probably imported from the Far East, where dragons are usually benevolent, mighty, and righteous.

Homer's dragon, painted on the shield of Hercules, the strongest man, represents: "The scaly horror of a dragon coiled full in the central field, unspeakable, with eyes oblique . . . that askant shot gleaming fire . . ."

Ancient poets like Philostratus elaborated on the dragon types even further, breaking them down into those who lived in mountain caves, as opposed to those who lived in marshes; those who had saffron-colored chin beards to those who were clean-shaven; and those who had crests to those who were otherwise bald.

A Middle Eastern dragon sighted near Jordan was so long that a cavalry regiment, separated by his bulk, could not see each other. Perhaps this is the reason that the Persians, Scythians, Parthians, and other Middle Eastern peoples painted dragons on their army banners. Soon, even the banners themselves came to be called "dragons," the origin of the

37

word "dragoon"—a specially trained army regiment.

King Arthur himself wore a dragon imprint on his helmet, as did the Anglo-Saxon hero Beowulf on his shield. Celtic knights of the Roundtable obeyed their chief, or *Pendragon,* to the extent of sacrificing their own lives in times of great danger. The killing of such an important chief in battle was reported as "slaying the dragon"—another way of keeping the monster myth alive.

Serious thinkers of the later Middle Ages exploited the myth for religious and patriotic reasons as well as for their interest in natural and unnatural history. Athanasius Kircher, a fourteenth-century German writer speaking of marvels, says:

> Since monstrous animals of this kind for the most part select their lairs and breeding places in subterraneous caverns, I have considered it proper to include them under the head of subterraneous beasts. I am aware that two kinds of this animal have been distinguished by authors, the one with, the other without, wings. No one either can or ought to doubt concerning the latter kind of creature, unless perchance he dares to contradict the Holy Scripture, for it would be an impious thing to say it when Daniel makes mention of the divine worship accorded to the dragon Bel by the Babylonians, and after the mention of the dragon made in other parts of the Sacred writings.

To reinforce their arguments, monks like Kircher pounded their readers with evidence from the clas-

7. *Dragons were popular in the ancient world. This nineteenth-century woodcut shows the German knight, Sigfried, killing a dragon.*

sics. Alexander the Great, for example, is reported to have come across an enormous cave-dwelling dragon who hissed so impressively that the entire army offered him food and worship. Strabo, another respectable Latin source, has documented such mountain dragons in a most lifelike and colorful prose. These are, he claims, the largest of all dragons. They are always scaly, gold in color, and bearded. Their arched eyebrows are enormous, their faces and their screams the most terrifying imaginable. Mountain dragons sprout bright yellow crests and bright carbuncles in their foreheads.

It is this last feature that is most interesting, for later dragon legends make much of this precious stone in the monster's forehead. Pliny, who ascribed magical properties to the dragon's skin, bones, eyes, and teeth, also comments on the precious stone usually lodged in its head. The Persian *Ganj*, or treasure guardian, is also a dragon. Eastern dragons are never portrayed *without* such a precious carbuncle in their foreheads. Here then might be the place where the treasure and dragon myths converge.

Recall Strabo's mountain dragon, with his scales of gold; or his dragons of the flat country who "differ from the former in nothing but having their scales of a silver color . . ." Silver, gold, precious stones, dark caves, supernatural beasts—these are the elements that treasure stories are made of. Could all this talk of dragons and precious hoards be nothing more than an allegory of man's timeless but fear-tinged desire to mine the earth for its wealth? Konrad Gesner, a pious sixteenth-century naturalist, thinks so. Dragons, he believes, guard treasure in myth because they symbolize "the danger of having possessions of great value."

To frighten themselves even further, men created monsters in places like Ethiopia, wild places where anything could happen—even dragons growing to thirty paces in length that could live for near a hundred years. Perhaps our ancestors gazed on the temple ruins of lost nations and imagined monsters like the Phrygian dragon who slept in the sun on a riverbank with his neck gently stretched out against the shore and his mouth conveniently open for catching stray birds with his great steamy breaths. To give them a more down-to-earth quality, some claimed that dragons are fearless of all beasts but the eagle, and that they hide at the mere flapping of the majestic wings. (Where, one wonders, does a thirty-foot monster hide itself?)

Dragons have acute sight and hearing, and it is in their nature to be grateful to people who have done them favors. Their appetites are unbounded; in fact, they gorge themselves. But, conscious of all nature's secrets, they are wise enough at least to suck the juice of the wild chicory plant as protection against gas before they eat fruit. When ready to feast on man or animal, they fill their stomachs with deadly herbs and roots—presumably to digest the meat faster.

Monsters

Cynoprosopi, a certain class of dragon that inhabits the Sahara, lives on goats and antelopes. These are black doglike monsters who shrill and hiss. Although equipped with dog's heads and otherwise normal dragon bodies, the Cynoprosopi are bearded, armed with sharp claws, and are hairy rather than scaly. Variety is, after all, the spice of life.

What has descended to us as the first drawing of our most typically imagined dragon was executed in 1598 in Switzerland. This monster with the long crocodile's body, scaly bat's wings, and long neck was believed to emerge only infrequently from its cave because the earth's surface was not amenable to its needs. Hence, scholars like Kircher argued, the few recorded dragons who had engaged in famous battles with famous heroes, were really blunderers, no more than lost dragons looking for the way back to their subterranean caves.

Sea dragons, on the other hand, live in great underwater castles where they feast on opals and pearls. Five such monsters hold up the oceans; the chief resides beneath the very center of the earth, while the other four princes are placed at each point of the world. The bodies of all five extend to three or four miles in length; their scales are yellow, their legs and tails shaggy. All wear whiskers on their chins, all have flaming eyes and jutting foreheads with thick small ears, big open mouths, long tongues, and sharp teeth. Should they feel like causing typhoons, the five sea dragons merely rise simultaneously to the water's surface.

Dragons, Basilisks, and Variations Thereof

Dragons are also reputed to be good swimmers. To get to Arabia (apparently a favorite dragon vacation spot), the monsters cross the Red Sea by coiling themselves together and forming a snake boat of sorts.

We must not forget the female dragon—or dragonette? One very dangerous hundred-foot creature of this type inhabited the Isle of Lango under the title "Lady of the Land." According to Sir John Mandeville: ". . . she lieth in an old castle, in a cave, and sheweth twice or thrice in a year, and she doth no harm to no man, but if men do her harm. And she was thus changed and transformed, from a fair damosel, into the likeness of a dragon, by a goddess that was called Diana." The usual knights happened along in an attempt to break the spell, but kissing the monster on the mouth proved too much of a test, and they all died. The "Lady of the Land" supposedly still sits and waits for her brave knight to this very day. That lucky man—should he survive the fatal kiss—will have a lovely lady, an island to himself, and plenty of money.

A much less attractive but even more powerful female dragon was Grendel's mother, "heroine" of the Beowulf saga. This aged underwater monster proved even more dangerous and nasty than her man-eating son, until Beowulf cut her to pieces.

More snake than dragon, a small species of winged, multicolored creature occupies the frankincense trees of Arabia. Herodotus, the Greek historian, has recorded the activities of these winged serpents in great detail. First, he notes that they are identical to the Egyptian winged serpent and that they can only be evacuated by styrax smoke. The Arabians interviewed by Herodotus believed that these winged vipers were so numerous that they might take over the world if not for the fact that the female bit her partner to death immediately after mating. The young vipers, in turn, avenged themselves on their mother by gnawing their way out of her belly and killing her in the process.

These monsters were shaped like the water snake, but sprouted bat's wings. The Egyptians held the ibis sacred because this bird was the mortal enemy of the destructive winged serpent. Each year, thousands of birds confronted the army of vipers in a deep gorge just outside Egypt, decimating them before they could enter the country. Cicero, a Latin writer, remarks later that ibises are useful in preventing the flying snakes from biting and spreading disease while they are alive, and from emitting infectious vapors when they are dead.

Modern Liberia is the setting for the *Mokélembêmbe,* another dragon. This vegetarian, elephant-sized creature will kill men without bothering to eat them. He is wingless, but possesses a long powerful tail, an equally long neck, and one long horn. Smooth-skinned and of a brownish color, this dragon is so bold that he climbs out of his river cave in search of food even in the bright light of day.

The reptilian dragon with the greatest impact on

Dragons, Basilisks, and Variations Thereof

the imagination of man has been the *Basilisk:*

> Beware, lest thou fall into my jaws!
> I drink fire. I am fire!—and I
> inhale it from all things: from clouds,
> from flints, from dead trees, the fur
> of animals, the surface of marshes. My
> temperature maintains the volcanoes:
> I lend glitter to jewels: I give colours
> to metals!

So cries Gustave Flaubert's raging Basilisk to Saint Anthony in the desert that its own fiery existence had created. The mere essence of the Basilisk could make birds fall down dead, cause fruit to rot, turn streams into poison and dry up. Its very glance was fatal not only to men and animals, *but to itself!* It was therefore hunted down by a man wearing a mirrored suit and a thick mirrored shield.

Like the scorpion, it loved deserts and sent men mad with its poisonous sting. Its hiss was sufficiently powerful to burn a man up with hydrophobia. Only the weasel could resist and kill this king of all dragons, which held itself erect and bore a precious jewel in its head. Only the crowing of a rooster could set to scurrying this monster with the fiery red eyes, pointed face, crested head, and white-striped body.

Otherwise called the *Cockatrice,* the Basilisk could only come into existence as the result of supernatural events. It had to be born of an egg laid by a seven-year-old cock and hatched by a toad during the days of the dog star Sirius. The egg itself was round rather than oval-shaped and had a tough outer skin instead of a shell. The creature, though essentially a snake, bore the traits of a toad and the comb of a cock. It was in the form of a Basilisk that the Devil came to tempt Eve.

THREE

MONSTERS OF THE DEEP

Paracelsus, a sixteenth-century philosopher and alchemist, expressed the commonly held belief of his times when he stated that sea monsters who resembled human beings bore the same relation to men as the ape, "and are nothing but the apes of the sea." Earth creatures therefore had their sea counterparts: horse and sea horse, dog and dogfish, snake and eel, spider and spidercrab, even monk and monkfish. Women named Jenny also have their counterparts in the ocean, for artificial "monsters," pieced together from various parts of the sea ray by bored sailors and then presented to gullible museum curators, were called *Jenny Hanivers*. Scholars have been unsuccessful in tracing the meaning of the name to a specific source, but falsified sea monsters remain "Jenny Hanivers" nonetheless.

Sea snakes, mermaids, *Krakens*—terrifying or vivid as they may be—are the least convincing of all monsters. Credulous ship captains, superstition, unreliable whales, and other enormous ocean creatures are

8. *The sea monster has often been used as an emblem of the Devil. In this illustration from a nineteenth-century book, a fisherman is trying to save himself from Hell by praying.*

responsible for all of our "evidence." These monsters vary little, most are long, reptilian, humpbacked, maned, and whiskered. Only the mermaid and merman really do anything other than frighten ocean travelers and turn over an occasional ship.

The *Ogopago,* a Canadian sea monster ranging from thirty to seventy feet, lives in fresh water, looks like a sheep with a beard, moves rapidly, and seems to do nothing of any importance to anyone. Like most other sea snakes or *sea orms,* this beast is related to Isaiah's apocalyptic Leviathan.

> In that day the Lord with His sore and great and strong sword shall punish leviathan, the piercing serpent, even leviathan that crooked serpent; and He shall slay the dragon that is in the sea.

Whenever events grew so terrible that the end of the world was feared, great sea snakes were sighted everywhere, but mostly off the coast of Norway—a favorite sporting ground for sea monsters. One report made by Hans Egede, "the Apostle of Greenland," runs as follows:

> Anno 1734, July. On the 6th appeared a very terrible sea monster, which raised itself so high above the water, that its head reached above our main top. It had a long sharp snout, and blew like a whale, had broad large flappers, and the body was, as it were, covered with a hard skin; and it was very wrinkled and uneven on its skin; moreover

on the lower part it was formed like a snake,
and when it went under water again, it cast
itself backwards and in so doing it raised its
tail above the water, a whole ship-length from
its body . . .

No doubt an imaginative churchman's watery version of that old vicious reptile himself, the Devil.

The years between 1820 and 1890 must have been equally troubled. This "end of the world" period saw the surfacing of the Great Lake monster, a creature with a smooth dog's head, lantern-sized eyes, stumpy feet (or fins), and ears like sails placed tight against the neck. Presumably, like Hans Egede's sea snake, this monster spent most of its time stealing unwary sailors from the poop decks of passing vessels. Most such sightings have taken place during July and August, a season of ocean calm around the Norwegian fiords. Witnesses claimed to have seen terrible struggles to the death take place between these monsters and whales, their natural enemies. One such July battle is documented in the records of the British ship *Pauline,* whose captain and crew submitted sworn documents to that effect on January 15, 1876.

A still more famous sighting had been made in 1848 by the captain and crew of the *Dedaelus,* who publicized their account in the London *Times* on October 9, 1848. The creature, which had passed in front of the ship's quarter deck with sixty feet of

9. *A nineteenth-century engraving showing what a real sea serpent is supposed to look like.*

its body in a straight line on the surface of the water, was described by the captain as follows:

> . . . an enormous serpent, with head and shoulders
> kept about four feet constantly above the surface
> of the sea, and, as nearly as we could approximate
> by comparing it with the length of what our main-
> topsail-yard would shew in the water, there was at the
> very least sixty feet of the animal . . . no portion of
> which was, to our perception, used in propelling it

51

through the water, either by vertical or horizontal
undulation . . .

The diameter of the serpent was about fifteen or
sixteen inches behind the head, which was, without
any doubt, that of a snake; . . . its colour a dark
brown, with yellowish white about the throat. It
had no fins, but something like the mane of a
horse, or rather a bunch of sea-weed, washed about
its back.

With the increase in monster sightings came a
spate of legends: sea serpents were allergic to castor
oil and *assafoetida,* an evil-smelling herb. This did
much to boost the castor oil trade, for Norwegian
sailors stocked up on it, throwing great quantities of
the stuff at the monsters, who would immediately
dive to the bottom of the sea to escape its noxious
odor. No monsters were reported to have died of
castor oil poisoning, however. Another belief was
that any sailor touching the sea orm's excreta would
be victimized by terrible swellings and bodily pain.
One great water serpent in Miosen on Hedemarken
reputedly foretold the death of the Norwegian king
and its effects on the country's politics. This is, admittedly, the only statement we have of a talking sea
serpent; all the others seem to have been mute.

Another Norwegian monster, a snake two hundred
feet in length and twenty feet round, frequented the
cliffs surrounding Bergen. This ambidextrous monster spent its moonlit nights devouring farm animals
on land or starfish and crabs at sea. Maned, scaled,

10. The Kraken was such a popular monster that he was sometimes put on maps. Here is a sixteenth-century chart of the North Sea showing a ship anchored to one of these gigantic beasts. Notice the two sailors who are cooking a meal on the creature's back.

and fiery-eyed, it occupied its leisure time raising itself like a mast, tossing ships around, and snatching those same unwary sailors from the decks again.

Olas Magnus, a chronicler of these sea monsters, describes a specifically Norwegian type, the Kraken. One is tempted to ask just how close the man got to this cruel sea beast who "frightens" and "amazes" men, and whose:

> forms are horrible, their Heads square, all set
> with prickles, and they have sharp and long horns
> round about like a tree rooted up by the Roots.
> They are ten or twelve Cubits long, very black
> and with huge eyes: the compass whereof is
> above eight or ten cubits: the Apple of the Eye
> is of one Cubit, and is red and fiery coloured,
> which in the dark night appears to Fisher-
> men afar off under Waters as a burning fire,
> having hairs like Goose-Feathers, thick and long,
> like a Beard hanging down; the rest of the body,
> for the greatness of the head, which is square,
> is very small, not being above 14 or 15 Cubits
> long; one of these Sea-Monsters will drown easily
> many great ships provided with many strong Mariners.

If land treasures are guarded by cave-dwelling dragons, then why not sea monsters to guard the treasures of the deep? Why should man, equally terrified of plundering the unknown seas for food as he is of mining the ores of the earth for wealth, not populate the ocean depths with malevolent monsters? Thus, among Norwegian fishermen there arose the belief that wherever the Kraken appeared there lay a full day's catch. However, when the water level changed in that spot, it was time to flee to a safe distance, for this signaled the rising of the monster himself.

Accompanied by a strong scent which attracted

other fish to it, the Kraken spent whole months stuffing itself to appease its voluminous appetite. For the rest of the year, it evacuated what it had eaten, leaving much of the surrounding sea muddy and rough. At death, its enormous carcass rotted quickly and putridly—one good reason, the sailors claimed, for its never having been brought back to the shore for examination.

Unlike the apparently useless Kraken and the clumsy sea snake, mermaids and mermen fulfill several convenient functions. First, according to Bishop Pontoppidan's *Natural History of Norway*, they sing very sweetly. Secondly, mermen possess the gift of prophecy and divine oratory. This belief dates back to the Babylonians whose fish-man god, Ea, came out of the sea to enlighten mankind two thousand years before the birth of Jesus. With his bearded head, scaly trunk and tail, Ea emerged from the waters at sunrise, instructed humanity in all the arts and sciences during the day, and returned to the sea at sunset. Such is the origin, too, of mermaids and mermen in India, Greece, and Rome.

Nereads, a type of young mermaid, have long green hair and fishtail bodies. They are closely related to the sirens who tempted Ulysses with their song and represent, from that time on, the sailor's temptation to madness during his long lonely voyages at sea.

Shetland Island mermaids spend their days in lovely pearl-and-coral underwater castles. Much more ravishing than human females, these creatures cover themselves in a *ham,* a fish disguise, and reveal themselves to fishermen as warnings of danger at sea. Should one of these ladies lose her fish disguise, she may never again return home, but must remain forever where she is.

So much like humans are mermaids and mermen that they shriek and cry when caught. Their flesh is said to taste like pork, their ribs provide a remedy for hemorrhage, while a certain bone in their foreheads dissolves gallstones when taken in powder form. Most merpeople are long, with oval-shaped heads and human features. Their foreheads are high and broad (which probably accounts for their superior intelligence), their eyes are small, but their mouths are large. Mermen and maids usually have flat noses, but they are minus chin and ears. Four webbed fingers at the end of each long, jointless arm comprise their hands.

Females have breasts and suckle their offspring; the sex of a merperson is distinguishable by the different generative organs of male and female. Merchildren (whose fathers need not be mermen) range from human infant-size to the height and weight of a three-year-old. Norwegian peasants have been known to catch these *marmaete* and take them home, where they feed them milk. The little creatures are in the habit of rolling their eyes about in surprise at their new surroundings before being consulted about the future. Once they have made their prophe-

11. An old engraving of a merman.

cies—during a period not exceeding twenty-four hours—the peasants feel compelled to return them to the sea, depositing them in exactly the spot where they found them.

12. The belief in mermen goes back a long way. Here is an ancient Greek picture of Hercules wrestling with a Triton.

FOUR

THE SYMBOLISM OF MONSTERS

All myths concern themselves in one way or another with human fears, wishes, and illusions. But they deal equally with the "monstrous" impulses that crouch within the shadows of the mind. Myths allow all kinds of wild behavior to symbolically take place; they are society's stopgap, you might say. Hercules, with his invincible strength; Nebuchadnezzar's impervious Sirrush; Isaiah's destructive Leviathan—each one of these represents the collective fear and aspiration of a people. Monsters are more "personal," as it were; they represent our own worst imaginings about ourselves.

Take the *Lamia,* for instance. Descended from Lilith, Eve's predecessor in the Old Testament, this monstrous female, rejecting her "womanly" function from the first, spends her time entering houses at dead of night, carrying off children, then murdering and eating them. Like the Devil, she is snake-shaped, outwardly seductive, and ruinous to the human race. The Hebrew myth has it that God, angered at her independent attitude (she refused to serve Adam), turned her into a whistling demon and substituted in her place the more docile Eve. (A mistake in her own right.) Clever serpent monsters like Lilith are so frequent in our history that they suggest a connection between human beings— the highest creature on earth—and the crawling reptile. Man, with one foot in the stars and the other firmly implanted in a mud puddle, reads his conflict literally in the image of the wise serpent.

Monsters represent the bizarre union of opposites —on the one hand they possess everything desirable: occult wisdom, great wealth, medicinal healing power, majesty, and strength. Yet they spit fire, kill at a glance, and toss huge vessels about like toys.

The hero must always conquer the symbolic beast in himself in order to gain the secret. The lowly scorpion of the zodiac is, on a higher level of existence, actually the lordly eagle. The struggle between our basest and noblest impulses is most poetically exposed in the man-beast combinations that proliferate every mythology since the beginning of time. We can, if we like, read it as a throwback to the point at which we branched off from the ape; a bit wild and shaggy still, but walking upright. Or we can, like the Christians of the Middle Ages, look upon *Satyrs* and *Centaurs* and *Sphinxes* as obstacles on a spiritual map charting our progress toward God. It works either way.

The Symbolism of Monsters

Starting with the wild man, we confront a lone creature who prefers caves and crevices to the open plain. He barely survives on berries and raw meat from the animals he catches and kills with his own hands. His shifty eyes are always alert against the dangers from real and imagined beasts which stalk him from behind the dense foliage, from the sky, from rivers and ponds. The wild man's legs are like oak trees, his body stooped and hairy; he has a terrible temper, makes hideous noises, and kills at the slightest provocation. Eating the meat of this monster's body is said to cure mental diseases, and his gall supposedly cures jaundice. Centuries pass, and the wild man, dressed in a suit, discards his wild ways. But with him he carries always the shadow of that earlier monster; intuitively awed and frightened by its continued existence, he allows his mind to fancy on it and, during his spare time, forges a harmless symbol of a dangerous living impulse.

Ancient art is filled with lion-jawed men and women, horse-men, bird-women, triple-headed figures with human bodies—every human and animal combination conceivable. Imagine a world still close enough to the wild man of the woods to remember its own savage past, and yet civilized enough to characterize its wilder impulses in animal figures. The Egyptians saw the Sphinx as a winged lion-man, the Greeks as a lion-woman; both attributed to it many supernatural powers. A composite monster born of fable and misty legend, the Sphinx set enig-

61

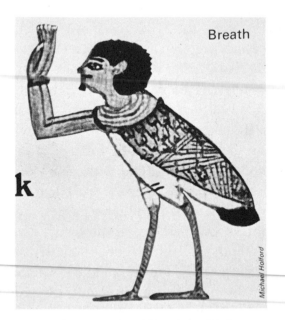

Breath

k

Michael Holford

13. *An ancient Egyptian bird-woman.*

matic riddles, then devoured whole towns of people who could not solve them. With her dog's body, lion's paws, woman's head and breasts, serpent's tail and bird's wings at rest, the Sphinx sat cruelly poised above the head of the terrified examinee and spoke her puzzle in a human voice. When at last Oedipus answered her riddle correctly, the Sphinx became enraged, dashed her head against a rock, and died instantly.

The Symbolism of Monsters

In this story we find the Sphinx used as an initiatory device that terrorized the unworthy with her complex riddles and was thus successful in guarding cosmic secrets. Once again, a monster has been used to protect something very valuable from the eyes of the profane. In this way, the ancient Pharaohs maintained the supernatural secrets that set them apart from the masses. So, too, Thoth, the hawk-headed man-god of Egypt, patron of magicians and writers, jealously guarded his secret knowledge from all but a brave few who became his high priests. Initiation into these mysteries could cost a man his life.

In Christian art, animals were used to symbolize various esoteric beliefs; this time, possibly, to keep the knowledge not only from the unworthy, but from outside persecutors as well. Early Christianity, like many other sects of the first century, had to wrap its tenets in symbols for protection. Thus, St. John is depicted with a tortoise head, St. Luke as a fox, and St. Mark in the shape of a lion. Medieval Christians continued the tradition, adding deformed devils and dwarfs, contorted demons with animal faces, mermaids, dragons, and the like because by then they had assimilated many of the magical customs practiced by indigenous European peoples like the Celts and Druids.

Pre-Christian nations—especially the Greeks—specialized in composite art of this type. Unaware of women's liberation, they had the peculiar idea that the most frightening monsters were human females with various animal features attached to them. *Hecate,* the first and greatest of Greek witches, for example, had three heads: a horse's, a dog's, and a lion's. Every night, surrounded by her disgusting entourage of spooks, all three of her emerged from Hell and tutored willing students in the art of sorcery. The whining and howling of dogs announced her arrival. Again, a figure designed to keep the merely curious away, Hecate stood for initiation into the secrets of nature, another name for witchcraft.

Three fabulous winged monsters born to Neptune and Terra (ocean and earth), also female, represent the misery of a guilty conscience. These *Harpies* have women's features and vulture's bodies. Their hair is always long, loose, and wild; they travel faster than the wind and tear at their victims with their terribly sharp claws. Unrelenting in their vengeance (we all know about a "woman's fury" and all that), they are the Greek emblem of punishment for the act of murder. Moreover, in keeping with the ancient idea of women as both morally and physically unclean creatures, the Harpies emit a foul stench and pollute the atmosphere around them with their presence.

The Latin poet Virgil depicts these monsters, giving them insatiable appetites which cause them to swoop down from mountaintops to plunder other people's banquet tables. Nothing can exterminate these creatures, and not all of the world's perfumes can cover the infectious smell of the excrement they

14. Here is a Harpy apparently carrying off an evildoer for punishment. An ancient Greek sculpture from the Tomb of the Harpies.

leave behind them after their meals. As if all this were not sufficiently frightening, Harpies screeched continuously, accompanying their attacks with an ear-splitting din. Enough to make any potential murderer think twice.

Monsters

Another nasty group of female monsters, Greek symbols of unadulterated violence, are the *Gorgons*. Stheno (the mighty), Euryale (the far-springer), and Medusa (the queen), the daughters of Phorcys and Ceto, were so ugly that a mere glance at them turned the unlucky viewer to stone. With snakes for hair, brass hands, scaly bodies, and wild-boar trunks, these beauties occupied themselves with challenging and conquering heroes. They met their match, however, in one Perseus, a man favored by the gods who had given him divine weapons for the battle. The story leading up to that confrontation runs as follows.

Once a very beautiful trio of sisters, the girls were turned into Gorgons because Medusa (the prettiest of them all) had defiled the temple of Athena (goddess of reason) by making love there to her boy friend, Poseidon. In a rather unreasonable rage, Athena turned Medusa and her sisters into the monsters described above. Poseidon, being a god himself, went scot-free.

(Classical Greek pictures of Medusa reproduce her head as a seal on coins and doorknobs. The face is always round, with large staring eyes, a cleft tongue that protrudes from the mouth, and scroll-like lines for hair.)

Apparently the monster was sufficiently annoying to King Polydectes, for that monarch personally enlisted Perseus as her challenger. Like all professional heroes, Perseus asked no questions but set about cut-

66

ting off Medusa's head and handing it over to Athena
—thereby exchanging furious impulse for reason. As
he rode through the air, however, a few drops of
Medusa's blood fell to the earth, turning into serpents as they hit the ground—in Ethiopia, of course.

From the same blood there immediately sprang up
a winged horse named Pegasus (poetry being the
child of unreason), who became a favorite of the
Muses on the spot. Pegasus, emblem of poetry, was
later given to Bellerophon, another hero, as an aid in
conquering the *Chimera,* a lion, goat, and dragon-
headed monster that spat fire everywhere indiscrimi-
nately. The horse evidently soothed the savage beast
with a song.

The Gorgon, a monster of the Underworld, therefore conveniently gave birth to the flying horse of
poetry—another metaphor embracing the typically
Greek ideal of harmony between wild earthy impulse
and noble-headed reason. But the Greeks were also
clever enough to know that a little wildness never
hurt poetry, and that even independent snake-women
like Medusa would continue to exert their fascination
on the world no matter how often you cut off their
heads.

Even the rugged cliffs that line the straits separat-
ing Italy from Sicily were regarded as monsters.
Scylla, the most dangerous of these, was once a
lovely sea nymph who had been changed by the
jealous witch Circe into a monster. Most natural
dangers seem to have been vividly identified by the

Monsters

Greeks in one way or another with women. For Scylla, in her new body, blasted ships and sailors with her six dog's heads, nine rows of devouring teeth, and twelve legs.

Cousins to Scylla, even resting perhaps in the crevices of her beastly protuberances, the *Sirens* are a group of deadly ladies who also live to destroy men. Sometimes they are half women, half fish, and sometimes half women, half bird. Sirens always have a horn at the crown of their heads, two wings, one bird foot, a knee with an eye in it, and human faces and breasts. Like mermaids, they have melodious voices with which they charm sailors, luring them toward Scylla's rocks, where they entice them to sleep with their sweet crooning. When the sailors are deeply asleep, these heartless monsters pounce on them and rip them to pieces.

Ulysses, the craftiest seaman of them all, had the wits to tie himself to the mast and stuff his ears with wax on his trip past the Sirens' dwelling. Undoubtedly this little picture was meant to serve as a warning to all unwary mariners against falling asleep at the stern, particularly while navigating the dangerous shoals within earshot of the wind's lilting echoes at shore. Nevertheless, we have every reason to believe that the Greeks were—despite all these poetic symbols—a women-hating race of men.

Amphitrites or *Apkallu*, the male fish-men, represent a happier side of the monster family. Evolved from Sumerian legends, these creatures have fish bodies and fish heads under which the man's human head is hidden (representing, perhaps, the mask and costume of an ancient wise man or high priest during his ritual performances). The voice was articulate, human in every detail when the monster addressed his human listeners. The Apkallu talked only during the day, when it fasted, teaching men the art of constructing temples, geometry, literature, and science. At sunset, he would plunge into the sea and sleep until the next day.

Although among the ancients male monsters generally emerge as more helpful than their female counterparts, there is an occasional Hydra to contend with. Born to Typhon (himself a misshapen man) and Echidna (half woman, half serpent), the Hydra had numerous human heads and poisoned breath which caused death and destruction even while the monster slept. Mostly confined to the depths of the ocean, the Hydra probably came about as a result of the Greek confusion concerning what we now call the giant squid.

The Centaur, half man, half horse, largely inhabited a country called Clyon. These monsters, representing rustic barbarity, or bad manners, dwell both on land and water, and feast on men. Lucretius, a skeptical Greek philosopher, claimed that the existence of the Centaur was an impossibility since men and horses live to different ages. Thus, he argued, a man-horse would find that one end of him had died of old age while the other end was still in its prime!

15. A medieval picture of a Centaur.

A more demonstrable insight into the origin of the Centaur comes from the pen of Father Stanislaus Arlet, a missionary in Peru in the year 1698. Writing of his encounter with the Canisian tribe, he says:

Having never before seen horses, or men resembling us in color and dress, the astonishment they showed at our first

appearance among them was a very pleasing
spectacle to us, the sight of us terrifying
them to such a degree that the bows and arrows
fell from their hand; imagining, as they
afterwards owned, that the man, his hat, his
clothes, and the horse he rode upon, composed
but one animal.

As usual, the Greeks postulated a more poetic origin for the monster; Centaurs, they said, were born
from the union of Ixion and a cloud, or—according to
another story—from Centaurus, a son of Apollo, and
Stilbia, daughter of Peneus. Because of their well-
known boorishness, the story continues, a tribe of
Centaurs were soundly beaten by the Lapithae,
whose women the drunken horse-men had violated
during a feast.

The name *Onocentaur* is a modern term designat-
ing a monster that runs on four paws and resembles
a huge monkey whose shaggy gray hairs are confined
largely to the lower part of its body. In Jonathan
Swift's *Gulliver's Travels* two variations on the Centaur monster are matched against each other. *Hou-
yhnhms* represent a fine group of horses with human
intelligence; while the *Yahoos* had thick bushy hair
on their heads, breasts, legs, and feet, wore beards
and went about with their bare brownish skin exposed. They both lay and sat on the ground, stood on
hind legs, and were excellent climbers because of
their fierce, sharp claws which could grip onto the
sides of rocky mountain faces. Like the Greek Cen-

taurs, these monsters were agile but rude country creatures that spoke in ugly guttural tones somewhat resembling, according to Swift, Dutch or German.

The Centaurs' Indian counterparts were monsters called *Silverstres,* wild men with hairy bodies, yellow eyes, and long pointed teeth. These unruly creatures communicated by means of horrible shrieks and could only be captured after having been made drunk.

While semihuman female monsters were usually regarded as emblems of punishment, it appears that ancient peoples looked upon their male counterparts as symbols of sin: Centaurs, as examples of drunken barbarism, and Satyrs as symbolic of unlawful and unlimited lust. Satyrs were old men of the woods who had the legs and tails of goats. In keeping with the evolutionary idea, these Greek semihuman monsters manifested outwardly whatever beastly mannerisms still remained within. Combining short horns and hairy goatish bodies, the Satyrs indulged themselves in girl-chasing excesses. They made their homes in dirty subterranean hovels, where they isolated themselves entirely from other humans and subsisted on uncooked vegetables. Although attempts were supposedly made to civilize them and to treat them kindly, these were always rebuffed by the intemperate Satyrs. (A throwback to the wild man of the woods.)

The Russian version of this monster is the *Ljeschi,* which is, in addition to its other obnoxious traits,

*16. An Etruscan bronze of the Chimera—a traditional
beast compounded of a lion, a goat, and a serpent.*

capable of changing its size and shape from that of the tallest tree to the tiniest blade of grass.

Classical animal monsters are usually artistic representations of mystery cults, magical formulae, official religions, political authority, and other state functions and ideals whose specific meanings are mostly lost to us now. We know, for example, that the Chimera, a lion-headed female monster with a goat's body and a serpent's tail foretold the danger of volcanic eruptions. In the Greek and Italian islands that comprised the hub of volcanic activity, it is no surprise to find the talismanic symbol of the Chimera on multiple palace doors, city gates, and temple entrances. Ornamentation with a purpose (usually a supernatural one) was a commonly used architectural device among the ancients.

Griffins, wild monsters imported from Egypt and Assyria, were believed to guard hidden treasures. They hated both horses and humans, never hesitating to tear either to pieces when they came across them. Half lion, half eagle, the Griffin combines the king of beasts with the king of birds into a symbol of majesty and strength that goes beyond all human considerations. The head of the monster features the eagle's beak, the paws are red, and the neck blue.

As guardian of all the splendors and eternal treasures of the universe, the Griffin is related also to the winged Assyrian bull, the Persian *Senmurv,* who united Heaven and earth, and to the Russian *Simargh.* The Christians have depicted St. Mark and

The Symbolism of Monsters

St. Luke as Griffins in many of their churches. Yet there exists some confusion amongst them, for the Griffin has at times stood for Christ and at others for the Devil. Isidore of Seville had no doubts, however, when he wrote: "Christ is a lion because he reigns and has great strength; and an eagle because after the Resurrection, he ascended to heaven."

Sir Thomas Browne, a man of more scientific turn, tried to identify the monster with the vulture, as a winged quadruped born wild in the mountains. As usual, Sir John Mandeville seems to know more about the subject than anyone else:

> . . . they have the body upward as an eagle
> and beneath as a lion. But one griffin
> hath the body more great and is more strong
> than eight lions, of such lions as be on
> this half, and more great and stronger than
> an hundred eagles . . . For one griffin there
> will bear flying to his nest, a great horse . . .
> For he hath his talons so long and so large
> and great upon his feet, as though they were
> horns of great oxen or of bugles or of kine,
> so that men make cups of them to drink of.
> And of the ribs and of the pens of their
> wings, men make bows, full strong to shoot
> with arrows . . .

Sometimes called the *Hippogriff*, but more related to the Sphinx than to the "hippo," the monster is characterized in *Orlando Furioso*, a courtly Renaissance epic, as a steed that:

Monsters

. . . is not imagined but real, for it was
sired by a griffin out of a mare: like
its father's were its feathers and wings,
its forelegs, head, and beak; in all
its other parts it resembled its mother
and was called Hippogriff; they come, though
rarely, from the Rhiphaean Mountains far beyond
the icebound seas.

Out of all the confusion about the monster's esoteric
nature and origins comes a clear and concise definition
by Lewis Carroll: "If you don't know what a Griffin is,
look at the picture."

Another monster that strayed out of ancient Egypt
is the *Phoenix*, a purple-colored bird that is identified with the sun. Living to the age of five hundred
years or more, the Phoenix is exactly the size and
shape of the eagle. Herodotus claims that its plumage
is really partly red and partly golden—yet it is not
the bird's appearance but rather its old associations
with immortality that makes the monster interesting.
To Herodotus, who claims to "give the story as it
was told me—but I don't believe it," we owe the following description.

[The phoenix] brings its [dead] parent
in a lump of myrrh all the way from Arabia
and buries the body in the temple of the Sun.
To perform this feat, the bird first shapes
some myrrh into a sort of egg as big as
it finds, by testing that it can carry;
then it hollows the lump out, puts its father
inside and smears some more myrrh over the

76

17. Here is a Phoenix about ready to burn up, as depicted in an early sixteenth-century manuscript.

hole. The egg-shaped lump is then just of
the same weight as it was originally.
Finally it is carried by the bird to the
temple of the Sun in Egypt.

A second version has it that the Phoenix, sensing
its own approaching death, builds itself a funeral

pyre, sets fire to itself, and burns to death. Nine days after the cremation, the bird rises up from its own ashes. Needless to say, it is this second aspect of the Phoenix story that has been most often identified with the resurrection of Jesus. As the Egyptians were, among other things, sun worshippers, we may also look upon the Phoenix as a metaphor for the sun, which appeared daily on the horizon, burned itself out by nightfall, and was revived again the following day.

Let us note here too that dragons who bear pearls on chains around their necks are also supposed to be carrying symbols of the sun. Within the pearl lies the secret power of the beast, another animal portrayal of the sun, which so many ancient people regarded as the source of immortal life. The Egyptians generally saw all natural events as fraught with supernatural importance. *Apis* or *Epaphus*, a magical calf, for example, was born whenever a flash of lightning touched a cow, causing her to conceive the prophetic monster, and after which she could never again conceive at all. Apis is known by its black color and by the white triangular mark on its forehead. The image of an eagle is imprinted on its back, the hairs on its tail are double, and it carries a scarab (another symbol of immortality) under its tongue.

Death, on the other hand, was always identified with frightening monsters who were out to do the victim no good; hence all the protective paraphernalia that accompanied a corpse to its final resting

Dogon

*18. One of the most frightening monsters of all—
Cerberus—the monstrous, three-headed dog who
guarded the entrance to the Underworld. Here it is
seen on a sixth century B.C. Greek vase. On the right
is Hercules who tried to tame the creature.*

place. One monster, an *Eater of the Dead,* was believed to appear to the deceased during the judg-
ment phase of his journey through the Underworld.
Assisted by the *Babai,* a Titan which had fathered
the Chimera, the Eater of the Dead (whose crocodile
head, lion's trunk, and hippopotamus' rear end were
designed to scare the dead man to death a second
time) leaped on a guilty sinner and devoured him
out of existence.

Monsters

Ugly monsters abound in the Greek Underworld. *Cerberus,* the three-headed dog that guards Hades, has a vicious temper, a filthy black beard, and clawed hands that rip at the souls of the damned. With his serpent's tail flapping behind him, Cerberus bites those who enter his domain as well as those who try to escape from it.

FIVE

FOREIGN AND HEARSAY
MONSTERS

An interesting fact about monsters is that they are always reported to live far from the writer's country. Sober-minded scholars like Polidorus, a fifteenth-century writer, have found no difficulty in accepting and transcribing a news item like the following:

> In the year 1496, was taken up out of the
> River Tyber, a monster having the tronke
> of the bodie of a man, the head of an Asse,
> one hand and arme like to a man, and the
> other of the fashion of an elephant's foote.
> He also had one of his feet like the foote
> of an eagle and the other like the hoofe of
> an oxe. The rest of his bodie with skales.
>
> He also had growing out behind him, a heade
> olde and hairie, out of which came another
> heade of the forme of a Dragon.
>
> It takes a glass of ale in his hand like a
> Christian, drinks it, and also plays at
> quarterstaff.

Monsters

Sensational pulp magazines and science fiction buffs continue to report the existence of such marvels even today. There seems to be an innate need in man for imagining wild creatures in inaccessible places. For us, however, even the moon which we have already seen with our own eyes on television, boasts nothing more monstrous looking than the weirdly clad astronauts themselves. And what ever became of the ever-popular "little green men from Mars"?

The difference between our situation and that of Giraldus Cambrensis, for example, is that we have access to television. All he had was a vigorous imagination and an audience both willing and able to suspend its disbelief. Writing specifically for medieval Christians, Giraldus emphasized the occult and supernatural aspect of monsters, their strange powers and effects on nature. Ireland and Scotland were "foreign" and still sufficiently pagan to harbor creatures like the *Banshee*. This invisible monster was believed to haunt at night the country houses of those about to die. Always female, the Banshee would set up a terrible howling and wailing under the future victim's window. However, since Banshees are invisible, we have inherited no description of them.

Giraldus also located in Ireland ordinary citizens with the magical power to turn anyone or anything into a red pig that could afterward be sold at the market. Perhaps this was his way of saying that the magical Irish would do anything for money. Another of Giraldus' reports deals with a man-monster whose extremities, eyes, and lowing voice were those of an ox. He ate by taking up his food with his cloven feet, and lived for a time at the court of Maurice Fitzgerald who had him secretly put to death. There is a lesson somewhere in all of this.

Xenophobia—or fear of foreigners—is also the motive behind Pliny's reports of the existence in northern Europe of the *Arimaspi*, one-eyed monsters who steal gold from the Griffins that guard it. To Pliny we also owe the description of "a race of men who have their feet turned backwards, with eight toes on each foot," who inhabit the peaks of a mountain called Nulo. Others, also mountain "people," have dog's heads and bark instead of speaking. Their enormous claws undoubtedly help them in hunting and killing the birds on which they are said to subsist. These *Cynocephali* are extremely bad-mannered, for they steal fledglings from eggs and eat them alive, in addition to blinding lynxes, evacuating from treetops on whoever passes by, crushing flowers wantonly, and violating women whenever they feel like it.

This sounds suspiciously like an unfortunate traveler's description of a hostile aboriginal tribe in full dress. So, too, the Ethiopian *Monocoli*, the agile one-legged monsters of otherwise human proportions whose single foot is large enough to put their entire body in shadow when placed between the supine Monocoli and the sun. Isidore of Seville calls them

Cyclopedes, whose one arm—which grows out of their breasts—they use for shooting their bows.

In his description, they hopped and leaped most gracefully on their one foot, but could also use their single hand and foot to propel themselves along in a circle when they grew weary of hopping! Also called by some *Skiapodes,* these umbrella-footed monsters spend their long hot afternoons tied to the earth by their long hair, and with their one leg in the air. "The light comes to us through the thickness of our heels," Flaubert has them say in his novel *The Temptation of Saint Anthony.* "No annoyances for us, no work! The head is as low as possible—that is the secret of happiness." To a later generation, then, Pliny's rather acrobatic one-legged monsters had become symbols of slothful mindlessness.

Not far from the Skiapodes, in that monster-populated country of the mind, live the *Troglodytae,* or aboriginal tribesmen whose Yemenite neighbors the *Nasnas,* offspring of the *Shikk,* are "without necks and have eyes in their shoulders," and have only one cheek, one hand, and one leg. These not-so-distant cousins of the Skiapodes are prized for the sweet taste of their flesh.

Forest people have always been looked upon as odd by "sophisticated" city folk. In eastern Libya, for example, European travelers claimed to have seen everything from headless men with eyes in their breasts (*Blemmyes*) to viper maidens with snake tails in place of human buttocks, to mouthless tribes who lived entirely on the odor of roast meat and flowers; not to mention the snake-armed, headless, and green-and-yellow men who lurked behind every bush and tree in the catchall land of Prester John.

Such natural "wonders" as talking parrots, the body markings and feature distortions imposed upon themselves by aboriginal tribesmen, pygmies, Watusi, and the like are magnificently elaborated upon by Sir John Mandeville, the greatest travel agent of them all. Mixing fact, strange custom, and fantasy all together, he informs his readers back home of the "many wild men that be hideous to look on; for they be horned, and they speak naught, but they grunt, as pigs. . . . And they speak [to their parrots] as apertly as though it were a man." To sharpen any flagging interests, Sir John also provides his readers with an ample sprinkling of dangerous monsters. One such treasure guardian is:

> . . . full horrible and dreadful to see, and it
> sheweth not but the head, to the shoulders. . . .
> For he beholdeth every man so sharply with
> dreadful eyes, that be evermore moving and
> sparkling as fire, and changeth and stirreth so
> often in diverse manner, with so horrible
> countenance, that no man dare not near towards him.
> And from him cometh out smoke and stinking fire and
> . . . much abomination.

On the nearby island of Dondun, there live the traditional thirty-foot-long, one-eyed giants dressed in skins who survive only on raw human meat and

the milk of giant beasts. These monsters have their
female counterparts, a race of cruel-natured women
with gems in their eye sockets who, like the Basilisk,
slay a man at a glance. Reminded of snakes by this
reference to the Basilisk, Sir John gives a delightful
prescientific portrayal of a hibernating serpent. This
monster eats no meat in winter, he says, which season
it spends lying in a trance. Once awake, however, the
serpent will kill and eat a man—weeping all the
while, as it moves its tongueless and chinless upper
jaw in chewing.

These marvels could be enjoyed simply for their
content, or scrutinized for whatever moral the medieval reader chose to select from them. One wonders, though, at the mental acrobatics needed to
make sense of the following anecdotes:

> On the isle of Pyten there are dwarfs who
> live by the smell of wild apples. And when
> they go any far way, they bear the apples
> with them; for if they had lost the savour
> of the apples, they should die anon. They
> be not full reasonable, but they be simple
> and bestial.

> or

> . . . there is an huge desert, wherein wild men
> are certainly reported to inhabit, which
> cannot speak at all, and are destitute of
> joints in their legs, so that if they fall,
> they cannot rise alone by themselves. . . . And
> if at any time, the Tartars pursuing them,

chance to wound them with their arrows, they
put herbs into their wounds, and fly strongly
before them.

And what is one to make of monsters who bark like
dogs after every two human words? Could this be
the sound of Bantu to the early European ear?
Surely the Moumoranian cannibals, who had dog's
faces and worshipped the ox, were caught in the
midst of a ritual and were wearing their ceremonial
masks when Sir John saw them carrying "the image
of an ox of gold or silver upon their foreheads" and
ransoming their conquered enemies, or devouring
them if the ransom was not forthcoming. Hairy prim-
itives abound everywhere, including those excellent
swimmers "who go as well under the water of the
sea, as they do above the land all dry. And they eat
both flesh and fish all raw."

In a reflective mood, we might muse upon what
our own descendants will say about *our* monstrous
tribal customs. After all, we too decorate our bodies,
slaughter our enemies, and consider raw fish a deli-
cacy. Only a foreign eye could call ugly or "foul
fashion" a lip so stretched out of size that it covered
"all the face." To the tribesman who spent years get-
ting it that way, the enormous lip is a distinct mark
of beauty. And what of a "folk that have the face all
flat, all plain, without nose and without mouth. But
they have two small holes, all round, instead of their
eyes, and their mouth is flat also without lips"? Cos-

metic surgery through the ages has adapted itself to changing standards of beauty: what one tribe calls a monster, another crowns and calls "Miss America."

Enviable traits, like the ability to communicate wordlessly, or to hear acutely, or to run quickly are transmuted into monstrous appendages. Pygmies hiss "as an adder doth," and "make signs to one another as monks do, by the which every one of them understandeth the other." An island people "have great ears and long, that hang down to their knees." Another island folk have horse's feet; while an extraordinarily nimble tribe—probably glimpsed in their traditional costume—is portrayed as going "upon their hands and feet as beasts . . . all skinned and feathered, and they will leap as lightly into trees, and from tree to tree, as it were squirrels or apes."

Certain primitive peoples whose men simulate childbirth in a process called *couvade,* are depicted as *Hermaphrodites,* that is half male and half female. Going a step further, Sir John gives each member of the tribe one female and one male breast and two types of genitals apiece. "And they get children when they use the member of the man; and they bear children when they use the member of the women." Thus, we see how symbols are transformed into monsters.

As a final justification for the existence of monsters on God's earth, Sir John concludes the reference to the fiends of Hell who intermarried with the Babylonian daughters of Nimrod and begot:

19. The Hermaphrodite, as found in a German book of alchemy.

Monsters

monsters and folk disfigured, some
without heads, some with great ears,
some with one eye, some giants, some
with horses' foot, and many other diverse
shape against kind.

But God's mercy is great indeed, for even monsters have the opportunity to be saved; as illustrated by the following fable.

A hermit in the Egyptian desert met a monster with two horns in its forehead, a man's body down to its navel, and a goat's body below that. Instead of attacking the Christian saint, the monster asked him to pray for it. As a reward for this request, the dead but redeemed monster's head and horns were the only relics permitted by the Pope to be placed on display at the church of Alexandria.

Pagan monsters have no such luck. The farther east you go, in fact, the less likely the possibility of Christian conversion. Indeed, Moslem monsters seem to exist for the mere sake of scaring people into calling on the prophet Mohammed. *Janns*, which inhabit the island of Jinn, scream so hideously that enough sparks, flames, and smoke emerge from their mouths to obstruct the path of the traveler. Persian monsters are admittedly illusions in many cases, but that does not make them less frightening than monsters in the flesh. Besides their bloodcurdling screams, Jinns possess the power to assume any animal form at will. As good an explanation of desert mirages as any that modern psychologists have yet come up with.

Foreign and Hearsay Monsters

That useful call to the prophet will scare away any *Div* (cat-headed man) or *Afreet* (horned and hoofed man) one might come across. Since demons commonly haunt the bodies of animals, no self-respecting Persian will kill a dog or cat. Because monsters are so related to the human family anyway, it would be inconsistent indeed to slaughter man's best friends. And with only a slight twist, any monster can be made friendly. Recall the three animal-headed apostles, Mark, Luke, and John. The Moslem version of the heavenly monster is *Burak,* a combination man, ass, horse, and peacock which bore the prophet Mohammed up to heaven on its back and thereafter came to stand for "divine love."

The Burak's opposite is the *Kujata,* a monster made up of four thousand eyes, ears, nostrils, mouths, and feet—all in the shape of a bull. Placed on the back of Bahamut (the Moslem Behemoth, or giant fish that holds up the seas), this monster is prevented from immediately devouring all of creation only because it is terrified of Allah's wrath.

Greek Lamias, *Minotaurs* (bull-headed men that fed on human flesh), and *Perytons* (wayfaring spirits of Atlantis who, although half deer, half bird nevertheless cast a man's shadow) were usually not connected with the gods except as characters in specific myths. These monsters were more symbolic of frightening natural events and less of religious meaning. Take *Acheron,* who is a perfect stand-in for a volcano. Bigger than a mountain, with flaming eyes and a mouth huge enough for cramming nine thou-

91

sand people into its depths, this monster is supported by two damned men who keep it forever propped open. Its three tunneled throats are perpetually belching fire; and its cavernous belly emits the constant wailing noise of its endlessly digested victims. Within Acheron's body can be found darkness, gnashing teeth, tears, fire, heat, cold, dogs, bears, lions, snakes—a familiar enough portrait of Hell.

There are frequent allusions in both classical and Christian literature to the *Mantichora*, a monster that seems to have died out after the sixteenth century. Wandering westward from India—that land beyond the pale where anything might happen—this man-eating lion with a human face, three grinning rows of teeth, and a scorpion's tail was considered responsible for spitting forth the plague. The bestiarists had a point there, for plague was often carried to Europe by the travelers who returned from the East, and the disappearance of the monster coincides with the tapering of the disease.

Artists couldn't make this dreaded monster sufficiently terrifying, so they padded, heaping detail upon gruesome detail: not only three rows of teeth, but each tooth sharp as a saw; gleaming blood-red eyes and a multicolored body—or, gray eyes and a red body; a man's face and lion's body, but at other times a man's body, the hairy fore and hind parts of a lion, the twisted claws of an eagle, a porcupine's quills, and a shrill, sibilant voice combining the tones of a flute and trumpet. Swifter than a stag, and

20. *The Minotaur was a Greek monster—a bull-headed man that fed on human flesh. This picture from a sixth century* B.C. *Greek vase, shows Theseus killing the Minotaur.*

issuing pointed darts from its tail as it ran, the Mantichora madly pursued its human prey. The Indians,
in self-defense, had already adapted themselves to
man-eating monsters like this one by evolving Pliny's
giant race whose eight-toed feet turned backwards
—in the opposite direction of the Mantichora, one
would hope.

During the latter part of the fifteenth century, an
age of exploration that opened all kinds of wild new
vistas to Europe, monsters sprang up as handily as
mushrooms. Conrad Wolffhart, a German monster
collector who lived from 1518–57, wrote of the existence of four-eyed men in Ethiopia and long horse-
necked men in Scythia. Paraguay still boasted a tribe
of men with tails ten inches long as late as 1885. And,
in his *The Romance of Natural History*, published in
1861, Philip Gosse notes that:

> On the cataracts of the upper Orinoco,
> Humboldt [an explorer] heard reports
> of a "hairy man of the woods," which was
> reputed to build huts, to carry off women,
> and to devour human flesh . . . Both Indians
> and missionaries firmly believe in the
> existence of this dreaded creature, which
> they call *vasitri* or "the great devil."

There are obviously a million and one variations
on the semihuman monster. But the scope of potential animal monsters is limitless. These range from the
purely destructive, to the simply marvelous, to the

morally enlightening, all the way to the everyday useful. It would simplify an extremely complicated subject to examine several of these categories separately. Merely "interesting" monsters are few and far between; people grew quickly bored with marvelous creatures who did nothing but groom their fourteen different heads and preen their rainbow-colored feathers. They wanted monsters who *did* something.

Under the branch of purely "natural history," we may place what Marco Polo called the *Elephant Bird,* an inhabitant of Madagascar. But this enormous bird-monster turns out, on examination, to be nothing but the ordinary roc, after all. Tiresome scaly monsters with donkey's heads and multiheaded elephants with webbed feet and eyes popping out of their stomachs probably made their way into Europe with the *Arabian Nights,* Alexandrian romances, and other mythological refugees from the East. One popular group of stories centered on a place occupied by a veritable zoo of monsters: two-headed wild geese, white lions the size of oxen, and "many other diverse beasts and fouls that be not among us."

But the search for the exotic was not enough to hold the continued attention of the increasingly literate reader. The spiritually inclined yearned for marvels with a message; scholars, alchemists, and witches longed for information about monsters that could be applied in their daily line of work. Such people would be interested, for example, in a Sicilian serpent that determined whether children were born out of wedlock or through lawful marriage. The manner in which the test was carried out was a bit severe, since the snake bit the illegitimates and merely skirted around the legally born; but people in those days had strong stomachs. Monsters like this Sicilian snake must have proved invaluable in deciding on questions of kingship and inheritance, for most noblemen had as many natural heirs in the family as legitimate ones.

In a country called Silba, where only crocodiles, snakes, and dragons lived, a certain four-legged yellow reptile growing upwards of eight feet, whose thighs were short and chunky and whose talons were long and spiky, guarded a deep lake comprised of the tears Adam and Eve had shed for their sins. Although no men dare live on this eight-hundred-mile-wide island, it is reported that magnificent pearls and jewels coat the lake's bottom, and that an occasional soldier of fortune will venture a dive. No statistics have yet been gathered on how many divers have reappeared on the lake's surface.

The shrewd explorer would do well to carry with him the ashes of a certain magical elephant which functions as an antidote to dragons, since nothing evil can approach the elephant's hair and bones once they have been burned. If this particular elephant is not available, the resourceful hero can substitute a friendly panther with a breath like allspice.

Allegorical-minded readers would automatically identify both magical elephant and sweet-breathed panther with Christ, who sacrificed his own body, descended into Hell, where he conquered the Dragon (Devil), was resurrected on the third day, and preached his great message to the world.

Those bold enough to travel through the land of Prester John are advised to carry with them the ashes of the *Leontophontes*. The remains of this moderate-sized monster will kill a lion instantly when placed on a piece of his dinner or at a crossroads where he travels. Lions hate the Leontophontes with a passion, and vengefully tear them to pieces when they find them. The only problem is that nobody has ever identified the Leontophontes, so that there is no existing description of the monster.

Practical types could fill their days searching for the *Crotote*, an Ethiopian monster born of a lioness and a hyena. Although it is reputed to inherit some of the hyena's magical properties, the Crotote leans more toward the interesting-but-relatively-useless category of monster. Its best trait is the capacity to mimic a human voice, but it cannot turn its eyes backward, and has one rigid toothbone that closes like a box. Its inflexible spinal column and gumless mouth probably make it unattractive to look at.

A white bird with a skull-shaped head, the *Caladrius,* was sought after by early physicians and magicians for its healing powers. The bird's dung could remedy eye troubles, but on a very good day the Caladrius might look at a sick man and predict the outcome of his illness. To those who would die, it turned its back; those who would survive were looked at full in the face. Then, assuming the illness itself, the bird flew toward the sun, where the malady was dispersed into the air. Noto the subtle relationship between the Christian Caladrius and the pagan Phoenix, which is also connected with the sun's healing rays.

Ninth-century Persians, who actually worshipped the light of the sun itself, believed that a three-legged ass with nine mouths and amber dung, whose single ears were larger than one thousand sheep or one thousand horsemen respectively, assisted the invisible powers of Life, Light, and Truth. The golden horn growing out of its head is hollow and sprouts one thousand smaller horns that will eventually destroy all the wicked of the earth. Poised in the middle of the ocean, although unseen, this white ass lives on spiritual food and conquers its enemies "through the keenness of its six eyes."

The line dividing a righteous monster from a purely nasty one is admittedly faint. One's reading most often depends on his country, his religion, his prejudices—or it may simply be a matter of taste. Briefly stated, one man's martyr is usually another man's Devil. The *Behemoth,* however, presents an exception to the rule. A biblical monster that crosses Hebrew, Christian, and Moslem lines, this floating hippopotamus-fish lives in a fathomless sea with no less than one bull, one ruby mountain, one angel, six hells, the earth, and seven heavens on its back! In

21. This old Sicilian mosaic shows a Phoenix whose head is sur-rounded by fire.

other words, three major religions have agreed that
Behemoth is the monster that upholds the world as
we know it.

Moslems, seeing in this monster a colorful allegory
for the cause and effect proof of God's existence,
have somewhat embroidered the original Old Testament Behemoth. Their *Bahamut* is so enormous, so
bright that man's eyes cannot look upon it. Its size is
such that if every one of the world's seas were placed
in one of its nostrils, it "would be like a mustard
seed laid in the desert." Bahamut lies above a sea,
which in turn lies above an airy abyss, which in its
turn lies above a blazing fire. At the bottom of all
this lies *Falak,* a serpent who bears all six hells in its
mouth.

The Middle East did not cease to present the
world with monsters, for as late as 1725 there is a report of a "terrible wild monster" killed near Jerusa-
lem. This creature comes down to us with not only a
full description, but a case history as well. Although
nameless, it is depicted as having been horse-sized,
with the head and teeth of a lion and the two horns
of a bull. A conglomeration of just about every animal
you can think of, it had an eagle's beak at the end of
its nose and eighteen-inch elephant's ears hanging
from either side of its head. Four dugs of a cow
dropped from its lion-skinned breast, and cock's spurs
grew along its back—all the way from its shoulder
bone to its feet. The monster's wings were large and

reptilian, and, to complete the picture, its entire body was covered with mother-of-pearl scales.

The legend behind its existence concerns a Tartar prince who wished to punish a group of people who had disobeyed him. Gathering them together on a pretense, he had these people brought to a mountaintop, where his henchmen murdered them by opening their veins. It was their blood, urged on by their unhappy ghosts, that merged with the earth and gradually evolved into this nameless monster of vengeance which tore men to pieces and drank their blood. "Vengeance breeds vengeance" seems to be the moral of this story.

A similarly gruesome medieval monster, the French *Shaggy Beast* was believed to have survived the Flood although Noah had excluded him from the Ark. Its snake head sat atop a bull-sized body covered with long green fur that hid its deadly stingers. A killer of both men and cattle, this perpetually angry monster had a serpent's tail and broad tortoise hoofs with which to stamp out its pursuers. Periodically, the Shaggy Beast would shoot out flames that withered crops, or it might raid stables at night. The unlucky farmers whom it terrorized would try to hunt it down from time to time, but that only created terrible floods throughout the Huisne valley, for the Shaggy Beast hid in the river's waters and caused them to overflow. An interesting simile for a terrifying natural event common to the Huisne valley.

Another indiscriminate devourer of men is the

Monsters

Leucrota, a donkey-sized creature with the haunches of a stag, the breast and shins of a lion, a horse's head, cloven hoofs, and a mouth big enough to stretch from one ear all the way over to the next. In place of teeth, the Leucrota had one continuous bone, and a human voice with which it presumably lured its human victims.

The *Yale* is a monster (created perhaps by a Harvard undergraduate) that reflects the evolutionary ability to adapt to its environment. In addition to its otherwise typical horse, elephant, and boar features, the Yale bears enormously long horns that adjust themselves to move about at will. "When it fights, it points one of them forward and folds the other one back, so that, if it hurts the tip of this one with any blow, the sharpness of the other can take its place." A relative of both the Leucrota and the Yale, the seventy-four-horned *Sadhuzag* has the ability to emit the loveliest as well as the most hideous sounds in the world. This is a fine example of how any monster may be attached to another, thus creating a third, theoretically, more frightening one.

The *Catoblepas,* however, falls into the category of the morally useful monster. A Greek word, meaning "that which looks downward," this fat and ugly creature is a black buffalo with a pig's head and a long, loose neck. With its pink, swollen eyes always lowered, it stares eternally at the ground through its mane of coarse hair. If it were to look up, it might kill whoever passes by with its wretched stare. Or, as

Pliny has put it: "Were it not for this circumstance, it would prove the destruction of the human race; for all who behold its eyes, fall dead upon the spot."

The *Unicorn* is a fascinating monster that falls into all possible monster categories: it is useful, destructive on occasion, and always interesting. Its great horn is reputed to be an infallible cure for nearly every known disease. Found in caves, this monster finds its way back to the Bible where, as the *Re'em*, it is described as having "great strength, an indomitable disposition, fierce nature, and an active and playful disposition when young." It was thus painted on the ancient crests of the kings of Israel, and came to be identified with the coming of a great man or supernatural savior of humanity. In its punitive role, the Unicorn is connected with punishment for the guilty and redemption of the good.

The Hebrew word Re'em was translated in the Greek version of the Old Testament as *Monoceros*, single-horned. In the fifteenth century, Photios, the Patriarch of Constantinople refers to:

> . . . certain wild asses which are as large
> as horses, and larger. Their bodies are
> white, their heads dark red, and their
> eyes dark blue. They have a horn on the fore-
> head which is about a foot and a half in
> length. The dust filed from this horn is
> administered in a potion as a protection
> against deadly drugs. The base of this horn
> for some two hands'-breadth above the brow,

is pure white, the upper part is sharp and
of a vivid crimson; and the remainder, or
middle portion, is black. Those who drink
out of these horns, made into drinking
vessels, are not subject, they say, to
convulsions or to the holy disease [epilepsy].
Indeed, they are immune even to poisons if,
either before or after swallowing such, they
drink wine, water, or anything else from
these beakers.

Travelers are often responsible for spreading monster stories—you will recall Sir John Mandeville,
Pliny, and Herodotus. The Unicorn was probably the
most popular monster yet discussed. Some trace it
back to the African rhinoceros, whose horn was supposed to contain the remedy for arsenic poisoning.
In Asia men valued the rhinoceros horn as the base
for a love potion. And finally, in that land of all
marvels, Ethiopia, it was said that the Unicorn was
valued by other animals, who would delay drinking
in a stream until the Unicorn had soaked its horn in
the water to purify it! It was here, too, that the Unicorn performed further wonders like leaping from
the highest precipices to escape its pursuers and
landing safe and sound on its single horn.

Babylonian bas-reliefs portray Unicorns dating
back to 600 B.C. Even Nebuchadnezzar, a seasoned
monster collector, found the Unicorn a fabulous beast.
And Pliny, in describing the Monoceros, gives it the
additional glory of having never been taken alive.
Christians claimed that the beast was so large that

22. *A nineteenth-century drawing of the demon Am-
duscias. He is shown as being half man and half Unicorn.*

Noah could find no room for it in his Ark; thus, it swam throughout the entire Flood, only occasionally resting the tip of its horn against the Ark when it grew tired.

During the Middle Ages it was believed that only a virgin waiting patiently in the woods could hope to tame the wild beast. Eventually it would come, lay its head in her lap, and sleep. Then the hunters could surround it quietly and capture the monster. In Christian mythology, then, the Unicorn came to represent the taming of passion.

Still, rumors about the medical value of alicorn (powdered Unicorn's horn) continued to persist; its antidotal qualities alone procured alicorn owners great fortunes in gold. Myths die hard; it was not until 1741 that alicorn disappeared from the pharmaceutical lists.

Although natural historians today have positively identified the Unicorn with a type of wild ox called *Bos Primigenius,* it continues to haunt the imaginations of artists, poets, and other dreamers. Because we possess no definitive description of the beast, we must rely on such as the following:

. Travelers to Mecca (1503) upon seeing temple images of the *Karkadann* (the Moslem Unicorn):

> This beast is of the colour of a horse
> of weasel colour, and hath the head like
> a hart, but no long neck, a thynne mane
> hanging only on one side. Their leggs are

thin and slender like a fawn or hind. The
hoofs of the fore-feet are divided in two,
much like the feet of a goat. The outer
part of the hinder feet is very full of hair.

This beast doubtless seemeth wild and fierce,
yet tempereth that fierceness with a certain
comeliness . . .

And from Julius Solinus', *Polyhistoria,* translated
in 1587 by Arthur Golding:

But the cruellest is the Unicorne, a monster
that belloweth horrible, bodyed like a horse,
footed like an elephant, tayled like a Swine,
and headed like a Stagge. His horn sticketh
out of the midds of hys forehead, of a wonderful
brightness about foure foote long, so sharp, that
whatsoever he pusheth at, he striketh it through
easily. He is never caught alive; kylled he may
be, but taken he cannot bee.

What emerges from this welter of Unicorn de-
scriptions? To begin with, all reporters agree that the
monster ranges in size between a kid and a horse. The
great horn that protrudes from its forehead is invincible, killing elephants with one thrust to the
belly; none would contest its ferocious nature. Of all
beasts, the Unicorn is described as possessing the
harshest voice. Yet, some say that it is gentle to all
but its own species, which it will fight to the death
regardless of gender.

Monsters

The Unicorn (or Monoceros, if you prefer) frequents lonely desert places, and remains calm and pacific during breeding season, when it is so docile that it feeds alongside its mate. But once the breeding season is over, he again resumes his belligerence and departs alone in search of prey.

Young Unicorns were brought to ancient kings who had them placed in entertainment rings and set them at each other in order to exhibit their prowess during combat. Yet, despite their warlike nature, Unicorns would jump into the laps of virgin girls like tame lambs awaiting slaughter.

In the nineteenth century Cuvier demolished all information regarding the Unicorn when he claimed that animals with cleft hoofs, whose frontal bones were always divided, could never have one horn growing in the middle of their foreheads. So much for the controversial Unicorn (who received no less than sixty-seven pages in one medieval *Bestiary*)— until a twentieth-century scientist proved Cuvier wrong. Grafting together the two horns of a normal young calf, Dr. Dove, an American, transplanted them to the center of the animal's forehead. Here, there grew one single straight horn. Along with this development there occurred an even more fascinating one; the adult bull grew even more powerful than other normal two-horned bulls, and thus assumed control over the entire herd. Nevertheless, it was at this point that he turned mild and gentle, as strong and confident as his legendary forebear. The Unicorn, as it were, lives on.

SIX

MONSTROUS ODDS AND ENDS

When monstrous humans and beasts grew tiresome, mythmakers turned to vegetables, fruits, and islands. From primitive beliefs like animism (that all things have souls, even stones and clouds) came the likes of the *Astomi*, monsters made of breezes that float along and are dissolved by darkness or rough noise. The Babylonians even went so far as to describe a grove of trees that bore human heads for fruit. Educated Europeans of the thirteenth and fourteenth centuries believed that a certain Irish or English island tree produced a fruit that became a bird and then a small wild goose. Christian monks convinced themselves that such geese were "not flesh nor born of flesh," and could therefore be eaten on Fridays and during Lent. Nevertheless, the high church council outlawed such "vegetarian" duck feasts in 1215.

Giraldus Cambrensis, writing somewhere between A.D. 1154 and 1189, describes these *Barnescas* in his *Topographia Hibernia:*

Monsters

They are like marsh geese, but somewhat
smaller. They are produced from fir timber
tossed along by the sea, and are at first
like gum. Afterwards they hang down by their
beaks, as if from a sea-weed attached to the
timber, surrounded by shells, in order to
grow more freely. Having thus, in process
of time, been clothed with a strong coat
of feathers, they either fall into the
water or fly freely into the air. They
derive their food and growth from the sap
of the wood or the sea, by a secret and
most wonderful process of alimentation.
I have frequently, with my own eyes, seen
more than a thousand of these small bodies
of birds, hanging down from one piece of
timber at the seashore, enclosed in shells
and already formed.

The Arabs combine usefulness with fantasy in their
version of the human fruit tree. Women, complete
with limbs, bodies, eyes, and generally beautiful
faces, hang by their hair from these marvelous
branches after having sprouted forth from large
brown leathery pods. Crying "wak wak" into the sun-
filled air until someone cuts their hair and sends
them crashing to the ground, these ladies represent
a bad omen for the future.

Not too far away from these fruit-women groves,
in Jaffa, there is a great rock that juts out into the
sea. Called Andromeda's Rock, where once a giant
sea monster had captured and bound a beautiful
princess, this natural wonder is still said to bear evi-

dence of a forty-foot monster rib. The author has gazed upon the rock, searching in vain for traces of a monster's rib; though none could be found, Andromeda's Rock remains an impressive sight as it stands.

Another Middle Eastern monster, the *Jidra,* was sought after for the magical powers inherent in its bones. Bones, monster or otherwise, have always been in great demand by those eager to forecast the future or place spells. Even dice, those unreliable forecasters of fortune, are sometimes called "bones." The Jidra was human in shape but grew from the soil like a pumpkin. Related to the European mandrake—another magical man-shaped "plant"—it was attached to its roots by an umbilical cord. Animals or men who might stray into the area where it grew were eaten immediately. Although attached permanently to the earth, the Jidra survived on nearby plants and, one supposes, on a sufficient number of wandering humans. In order to kill this valuable monster, one was advised to pull its umbilical cord, thus severing it from the earth. Sharpshooters were advised to cut it from afar with arrows. In either case, the Jidra was said to scream.

Seventeenth-century English writers like John Donne believed in the magical properties of the mandrake, an evil-tempered little plant-man that could only be picked on astrologically propitious nights and dumped into a sack. And even then the mandrake would squeal and holler. Health food and herb shops today still feature mandrake root or powder; only they call it *ginseng*, and import it from Korea and Japan. A cousin of the Middle Eastern Jidra, and closely akin to the mandrake, ginseng is supposed to keep one from growing old.

But all this takes us far afield from what we have come to think of as *genuine* monsters. You will recall the scales, bat's wings, fire-breathing snouts, and such. Human monsters aren't really monsters in the Frankenstein sense unless they carry a gruesome tale with them. Animal monsters, as we have seen, are largely symbolic representations of something or other out of the past. Krakens, mermaids, and the like have in our time grown less interesting and certainly less frequent than the talking dolphin or the performing seal. And for those of us brought up in the industrial West, dragons live on in fairy tales and emerge only to ply their trade during Chinese New Year celebrations.

What, then, is left? What can we genuinely call a monster today? Perhaps the following account of a *thing* sighted now and then in the southern part of the United States will revive our jaded imaginations and once again make our skins crawl.

This modern fire breather is ten feet tall and has a bright green body, round blood-red noseless face, and no mouth. Its eye openings project greenish orange light beams; its head is surrounded by a dark hoodlike shape that ends in a point. The monster, which waddles along in a combination bounce-float motion, lights itself up from the depths of its flabby body. Needless to say, it has terrible claws.

Monstrous Odds and Ends

True to monster form, this unnamed creature does little else than terrify occasional adult humans, dogs, and small children. No one actually knows whether its bones or hair or teeth are useful in curing lumbago, dropsy, or a broken heart. Even the state police haven't ventured a guess on that subject. Not one "witness" has ever gotten close enough to the monster to snap its picture. There have as yet sprung up no accounts of its mysterious origins in the land of Prester John—outer space seems more likely. We aren't even sure if the monster emits hideous shrieks, or if it sings sweetly; we don't know whether it prefers blond to dark-haired maidens, or if it might prophesy for us. All we do know at this point is that it is ugly, frightening, and dangerous—and that makes it a monster.

BIBLIOGRAPHY

Borges, Jorge Luis, *The Book of Imaginary Beings*, trans. by Norman di Giovanni, New York: Avon, 1969.

Brown, Sir Thomas, *Selected Writings*, Sir Geoffrey Keynes, ed., Chicago: University of Chicago Press, 1968.

Cohen, Daniel, *A Modern Look at Monsters*, New York: Dodd, Mead & Co., 1970.

Gosse, Philip, *The Romance of Natural History*, Philadelphia: J. B. Lippincott & Co., 1875.

Gould, Charles, *Mythical Monsters*, London: W. H. Allen & Co., 1886.

Hamel, Frank, *Human Animals*, New York: University Books, 1969.

Herodotus, *The Histories*, Baltimore: Penguin Books, Inc., 1954.

Willy Ley's Exotic Zoology, New York: Viking Press, Inc., 1959.

Pliny, *Natural History*, Loyd Haberly, ed., New York: Ungar Publishing Co., 1957.

Pontoppidan, Erik, *The Natural History of Norway*, London: Folio, 1755.

Bibliography

Thompson, C. J. S., *The Mystery and Lore of Monsters*, New York: University Books, 1968.

The Travels of Sir John Mandeville, New York: Dover Publications, Inc., 1964.

White, T. H., *The Bestiary*, New York: Capricorn Books, 1960.

INDEX

Index

118

Index

Index

Index

Satan, 33. *See also* Devil, the
Satyrs, 25, 60, 72, 73
Scarab, 78
Scotland (Scots), 20, 82
Scylla, 67–68
Scythia(ns), 37, 94
Sea monsters (sea serpents), 42–43, 47–58, 60 (*see also* specific monsters, places); *ill.*, 4, 51, 53
Sea orms, 49, 52
Sea ray, 47
Senmurv, 74
Shaggy Beast, the, 101
Shetland Island mermaids, 55–56
Shikk, 84
Sicily, 95–96, 99
Siegfried (*ill.*), 39
Silba, 96
Silvestres, 72
Simargh, 74
Sin, monsters and symbolism of, 33, 72
Sirens, the, 68; described, 68; *Ulysses* and, 68
Sirius (dog star), 46
Sirrush (Babylonian dragon), 35, 59; described, 35
Skiapodes, 84
"Slaying the dragon," 38
Snakes, 13, 34, 47, 49–55 (*see also* Sea monsters [sea serpents]; specific kinds, monsters, places); *ill.*, 51, 53, 86
Solinus, Julius, 107
Spain, dwarfs kept in the royal court of, 26
Sphinxes, 60, 61–63; described, 61–62
Spriggans, 20
Stars, Babylonian belief in appearance of monsters and position of, 18
Stheno, 66
Stilbia, 71
Stiles, Ezra, quoted on legendary Indian giant, 20
Strabo, quoted on mountain dragons, 40
"Strong lady," the, 23
"Strong man," the, 23

Sumerian legends, Amphitrites evolved from, 68–69
Sun, the, monsters and symbolism of, 78, 98
Swift, Jonathan, 71–72
Switzerland, 42
Symbolism of monsters, 14, 34, 35–36, 40–41, 59–80. *See also* specific aspects, kinds, monsters

Temptation of Saint Anthony, The (Flaubert), 84
Terra, harpies as children of Neptune and, 64
Terragus, 20
Thor (*ill.*), 4
Thoth, 63
Titans, 18–19, 79; described, 18–19
Tomb of the Harpies, 65
Topographia Hibernia (Giraldus Cambrensis), 109–10
Treasure-guarding monsters, 13, 34, 35, 40–41, 54, 62–63, 74–75, 85. *See also* specific kinds, monsters, places
Treves, Dr. Frederick, 29–31
Triton (*ill.*), 58
Troglodytae, 84
Tycho Brahe. *See* Brahe, Tycho
Typhon, 69
Typhoons, see dragons and, 42

Ulysses (Odysseus), 16, 18, 55, 68; *ill.*, 16
Unicorns, 103–8; described, 103–8

Velasquez, paintings of dwarfs by, 26
Virgil, description of harpies by, 64
Vitelli, Cardinal, 26
Vultures, 75

Weasels, 45
Welsh, the, 20
Whales, 50
"Wild creature" from Bilboa, 24
Wild men, 24, 61, 72, 86–87

Index

PERLE EPSTEIN is the author of a book called *The Private Labyrinth of Malcolm Lowry: Under the Volcano and the Cabbala* as well as *The Way of Witches* and *Individuals All*. She enjoys writing about occult subjects in spite of her academic background (she has a Ph.D. in English and Comparative Literature and is presently teaching a course at New York University) and believes that she inherited her interest in magic and mysticism from a Cabalist ancestor named Israel Bal Shem Tov—"Master of the Holy Name."

Mrs. Epstein is particularly interested in Yoga and Oriental philosophy, and highly recommends the head stand as a stimulus to writing.